David Walliams

DAVID WALLIAMS:
Britain's Top Talent

'I WANTED TO MAKE PEOPLE LAUGH.'

David Walliams is a highly successful comedian, writer, actor and television presenter. His distinctive brand of humour has made him one of Britain's most popular entertainers. As well as being a top-selling children's writer, David makes time to raise huge amounts of money for charity through amazing sporting achievements.

DAVID WALLIAMS

A Comic Genius

993802000 3

This paperback edition published in 2016
First published in hardback in 2015

Copyright © Wayland 2015

Editor: Elizabeth Brent

Produced for Wayland by Calcium
All rights reserved.
Dewey Number: 791.4'5'028'092-dc23
ISBN: 978 0 7502 9051 7
E-book ISBN: 978 0 7502 9050 0
10 9 8 7 6 5 4 3 2 1

MIX
Paper from responsible sources
FSC
www.fsc.org
FSC® C104740

Wayland
An imprint of
Hachette Children's Group
Part of Hodder & Stoughton
Carmelite House
50 Victoria Embankment
London EC4Y 0DZ

An Hachette UK Company
www.hachette.co.uk

www.hachettechildrens.co.uk

Picture acknowledgements:

Key: b=bottom, t=top, r=right, l=left,
m=middle, bgd=background

Cover: Getty Images: Dave Hogan (inset); Shutterstock: Featureflash
(main). **Inside:** Corbis: Rune Hellestad 17, Axel Koester 13, Reuters/
Paul Hackett 24, 25, James Whatling/Splash News 18t, 19; Getty
Images: David M. Benett 5, 6, 23, Mark Cuthbert 16, Carrie
Davenport 20b, Jon Furniss 30, Dave Hogan 8, Bryn Lennon 7, Danny
Martindale 14, 22, Karwai Tang 20t; Rex Features: Tom Dymond/
Comic Relief 21, FremantleMedia Ltd 11, Brian Rasic 10; Shutterstock:
Simon Burchell/Featureflash 27, Henry Harris/Featureflash 1, 2, 9,
Magicinfoto 15, Steve Vas/Featureflash 4, 29; Wikimedia Commons:
Allan Warren 18b.

NAME: David Edward Walliams (born Williams)

BORN: 20 August 1971

HOMETOWN: Merton, London

EDUCATION: Collingwood Boys' School, Wallington; Reigate Grammar School; Bristol University

OCCUPATION: Actor, writer, comedian, television presenter, charity fundraiser

FAMOUS FOR: Acting in Little Britain, swimming part of the River Thames for charity, writing children's books including Gangsta Granny and being a judge on television talent show, Britain's Got Talent.

LIKES: James Bond books and films

Did You Know?

David's surname was originally Williams, but he changed it to Walliams to get his Actor's Equity card – at the time, there was another actor with the same name and it helps to avoid confusion if actors have different names.

Early Spark

David's dad, Peter, was a civil engineer for London Transport. His mum, Kathleen, was a laboratory technician. Peter and Kathleen had two children – Julie and David. The family lived in Surrey, and Kathleen still lives in the house in which David and his sister Julie grew up.

One of David's favourite television programmes as a child was *Dr Who*. In those days, the Doctor was played by actor Tom Baker. Many years later, David was thrilled when Tom agreed to do the voice-over for his television show *Little Britain*.

DAVID, HIS MUM AND HIS SISTER AT A PERFORMANCE OF JOSEPH AND THE AMAZING TECHNICOLOUR DREAMCOAT IN 2007.

Walliams' World

Julie is two years older than David. She and David used to play together, dressing up in outfits from their dressing-up box. They also used to argue, like most brothers and sisters! Today, Julie is a primary school teacher.

DAVID AND HIS PARENTS ATTEND THE BBC SPORTS PERSONALITY OF THE YEAR AWARDS IN 2006.

David's first experience of being on stage was as Father Christmas in a school play, aged five. However, it was while he was at Reigate Grammar School that David realised he could act and make people laugh – and he loved it!

He was cast in a school play, *All the King's Men*, as Queen Henrietta Maria, wife of King Charles I. Dressed in a long, flowing dress, David's part was a non-speaking role, but he still managed to create quite a stir! Sitting on stage, surrounded by his 'ladies-in-waiting', the young David regally fanned himself, enjoying the audience's laughter. David had found his talent!

DAVID, SPEAKING ABOUT HIS EARLY LOVE OF PERFORMING:

'I WAS DEFINITELY THINKING, "OH RIGHT, THAT'S WHAT I WANT TO DO. I WANT TO GET ON THE STAGE AGAIN." THE ENGLISH TEACHER WHO ASKED ME TO BE IN THE PLAY PROBABLY SAW ME ACTING UP IN HIS ENGLISH LESSON AND THOUGHT, "OH YES, HE'S GOT A LITTLE SPARK OF THE PERFORMER ABOUT HIM".'

School Days

David's parents had saved up so they could send their son to a fee-paying school, Reigate Grammar.

He didn't always feel that he fitted in at school, and it took some time for David to find his confidence there. Despite this, he showed glimmers of the many talents he is so famous for today, including writing and performing.

David also enjoyed swimming, particularly long distances, and was eventually selected for the school team. David's love of the sport would help him to achieve great feats for charity in 2006 and 2011.

IN 2011, DAVID SWAM 225 KM OF THE RIVER THAMES TO RAISE MONEY FOR CHARITY.

David's favourite teacher at school was George Paxton, his English teacher. Mr Paxton taught David Shakespeare, and encouraged him to pursue acting. He was also very funny, and his classes were the highlight of David's week.

It was at Reigate Grammar that David began to find his comic voice and love of writing. Once a term, each class had to prepare an assembly. David grabbed the opportunity, writing funny spoofs of television shows to perform with his classmates.

'I WANTED TO USE THE ASSEMBLIES TO STAGE MY OWN COMEDY SKETCHES.'

IN A REVIEW OF THE PILGRIM, ONE OF DAVID'S SCHOOL PLAYS, HIS TEACHER STATED:

'THE PLAY PROVIDED A GOOD VEHICLE FOR PARADING THE AMPLE TALENTS OF ... DASHWOOD AND WILLIAMS.' [ROBIN DASHWOOD WAS DAVID'S BEST FRIEND].

David Walliams

Camp David
The Autobiography

Walliams' World

David began an alternative school magazine called *Wall Scrawl*, in which he and some friends wrote reviews of films and days out. They sold the magazine for 25p a copy.

DAVID IS NOW A SUCCESSFUL CHILDREN'S AUTHOR, AND HAS ALSO WRITTEN A FRANK AUTOBIOGRAPHY CALLED CAMP DAVID.

Growing UP

A quick wit and way with words earned David a place in the school's public speaking competition, in which young people made speeches, answered questions and took part in debates. David went on to win other debating and public speaking competitions for Surrey County.

As a teenager, star-struck David hung around stage doors, hoping to get an autograph from his heroes, including comedian Frankie Howerd. More than 20 years later, not only is David now signing autographs for his own fans, but he also appeared as Frankie Howerd in a television drama in 2008!

DAVID OVERCAME HIS SHYNESS, AND IS VERY CONFIDENT ON STAGE. IN 2003, HE AND MATT LUCAS DRESSED UP AS EMINEM AND CHARLOTTE CHURCH AT THE BRIT AWARDS.

DAVID ON PLAYING FRANKIE HOWERD:

'IT'S QUITE WEIRD HOW LIFE CAN BE SO CIRCULAR. I MEAN, IT'S JUST ODD TO BE A REAL FAN OF SOMEONE AND THEN 20 YEARS LATER TO BE PLAYING THEM.'

David has always enjoyed making people laugh but he was shy as a child. He didn't even like having his picture taken.

DAVID'S LOVE OF ACTING HAS CONTINUED INTO ADULTHOOD. IN 2002, HE APPEARED IN TV SHOW THE BILL.

DAVID ON HIS ENGLISH TEACHER AT REIGATE GRAMMAR SCHOOL:

'MR PAXTON SAW MY PASSION AND TOOK A SPECIAL INTEREST IN ME AND WE WOULD TALK ONE ON ONE. PERHAPS HE SAW ME AS A KINDRED SPIRIT. HE GAVE ME THE CONFIDENCE TO PURSUE MY DREAM OF BEING AN ACTOR WHEN I LEFT SCHOOL.'

Taking to the Stage

The young David was bitten by the acting bug and he wanted to do more. In 1989, he was finally successful in joining the prestigious National Youth Theatre (NYT), a theatre group that met during the summer holidays. During these times, David went to stay in London to devise and act in plays with other NYT members. He got on well with his fellow students – bonding with them over their shared love of drama and the theatre.

> DAVID, SPEAKING ABOUT HIS TIME AT THE NYT:
>
> 'FINALLY ... I WAS NOW WITH PEOPLE WHO HAD THE SAME PLAYFUL SIDE TO THEM THAT I HAD.'

David worked hard at school, and got the grades he needed for Bristol University, where he went to study drama in 1989. In his first year, he was delighted to be given the comic role of Bottom in a production of Shakespeare's *A Midsummer Night's Dream*. Years later, David played the role again in London's West End.

One of David's most famous and successful working partnerships has been with comedian and actor Matt Lucas. The two met at the NYT when Matt joined the group in the summer of 1990. Their first meeting was not a success, and the two men did not get on. However, within a year the young actors were working together again in a NYT production of Shakespeare's *The Tempest*. This proved to be the beginning of a long and successful partnership.

DAVID AND MATT HAVE WON NUMEROUS AWARDS FOR THEIR WORK.

Walliams' World

David kept himself busy while at university and had numerous jobs to earn money. During his summer holidays he worked in theatres, selling programmes and ice creams, and showing people to their seats.

DAVID ON MATT:

'WHAT BONDED MATT AND I WAS OUR LOVE OF COMEDY. WE WERE BOTH FANS.'

Funny Guy

David's reputation as a comedian developed during his final years at school. In 1988, he took over a school assembly for the charity Comic Relief, and his comedy routine raised more than £500. Speaking about the experience, David said, 'I was monumentally proud and eager to do more.'

Other sixth formers at his school would pay David to perform stand-up comedy at their parties. This was the beginning of David's work on the comedy circuit.

DAVID IS FRIENDS WITH MANY OTHER HIGH-PROFILE BRITISH COMEDIANS, INCLUDING JIMMY CARR, PICTURED HERE IN 2014.

While at university, David started a comedy night with a couple of fellow students. On the strength of this, one of his comedy partners, Jason Bradbury, managed to get the pair an audition with the BBC, but unfortunately they were unsuccessful.

David realised that if he wanted to make a living out of being funny, he needed to work hard. He studied other comedians and his comic heroes, such as Rowan Atkinson, in order to work out what made them funny, and what didn't work in their sketches or routines.

> DAVID SPEAKING OF HIS INFLUENCES:
>
> 'THE PEOPLE YOU LOVED AS A KID, YOU'RE ALWAYS IN AWE OF... IT'S NOT NECESSARILY ABOUT THEM BEING THE MOST FAMOUS PERSON IN THE WORLD, IT'S MORE ABOUT WHAT THEY MEAN TO YOU.'

Walliams' World

As a teenager, David got the chance to meet his comic hero, Rowan Atkinson, after waiting outside the stage door where Atkinson had been performing. As well as getting Atkinson's autograph, David asked him for advice on how to be a successful comedian. All Atkinson jokily said was "Don't do it!"

ROWAN ATKINSON WAS ONE OF DAVID'S INSPIRATIONS.

Working HARD

For a while, David and fellow comedian Jason Bradbury toured comedy venues with their double-act called Bunce 'n' Burner. They were very determined but not very successful!

In the early 1990s, David got a job as a runner on a television show called *Games Master*. He was then cast as the presenter in the BBC children's television series *Incredible Games*.

In 1994, David started writing for Ant and Dec, who were then two up-and-coming television presenters starring in *The Ant & Dec Show*. David would later work alongside the duo when he was a presenter on the highly popular television programme, *Britain's Got Talent*.

ANT AND DEC WORKED WITH DAVID BEFORE HE WAS SUPER-FAMOUS.

In 1995, David and Matt Lucas decided to work together as a comedy double-act. One of their first projects together was performing at the Edinburgh Festival, a three-week-long festival showcasing different drama and comedy acts.

The pair continued to tour their comedy show as well as taking on small acting parts. Eventually, their partnership resulted in a spoof interview show called *Rock Profile*, which was first shown on television in 1999.

Matt and David continued their collaboration, and in 2001, they recorded the first of two series of *Little Britain* for BBC's Radio 4. This later transferred to BBC television in 2003. The series involved sketches featuring exaggerated and eccentric characters from everyday life. David and Matt played most of the roles themselves.

Little Britain was hugely successful and won numerous awards, making the two men household names.

DAVID AND MATT, IN COSTUME AS LOU AND ANDY, AT THE LAUNCH OF THEIR LITTLE BRITAIN BOOK IN 2004.

ON WINNING A BAFTA AWARD IN 2005 FOR *LITTLE BRITAIN*, DAVID SAID:

'WE'D REALLY LIKE TO THANK THE BBC WHO HAVE BELIEVED IN US FOR MANY YEARS, EVEN WHEN WE WERE RUBBISH.'

Walliams' World

David has joined forces with comedian and actress Miranda Hart and comedy director Jo Sargent to set up a production company called King Bert Productions. Their aim is to develop their own work alongside offering opportunities to new and young writers.

David and Matt followed *Little Britain* with the spoof airport documentary series *Come Fly With Me*. Since then, Matt has gone to work in the United States.

Acting a Part

From his first appearance in a school play, David has always loved acting, and has proved himself to be a serious actor both on stage and on television.

The television series of *Little Britain* was so successful that a live show soon followed, which the duo took on tour around Britain.

DAVID LOVES PLAYING TO A CROWD!

David's acting roles have included playing comedian Frankie Howerd in the television biopic *Rather You Than Me*, acting in Harold Pinter's stage play *No Man's Land* and playing the comic character 'Bottom' in Shakespeare's *A Midsummer Night's Dream* at the Noël Coward Theatre in 2013. David both writes and stars in the television series *Big School*, set in a secondary school.

FRANKIE HOWERD

One of David's more recent jobs is as a judge on *Britain's Got Talent*. The audience love his engaging personality and sense of fun. David even gets up on stage, singing and dancing with some of the acts!

DAVID WITH SIMON COWELL, THE CREATOR AND CO-PRESENTER OF BRITAIN'S GOT TALENT.

DAVID'S MUM, KATHLEEN, THINKS HIS LOVE OF BEING ON STAGE AND PERFORMING COMES FROM HIS SHYNESS AS A CHILD:

'YOU WERE QUITE SHY IN LOTS OF WAYS. YOU WEREN'T THE OUTGOING PERSON THAT YOU ARE NOW. I THINK THAT'S WHY YOU LIKE WHAT YOU DO. WHEN YOU'RE ON STAGE, YOU'RE NOT YOURSELF, ARE YOU? YOU'RE SOMEBODY ELSE.'

A Public Face

Since the success of Little Britain, David has become a much loved and familiar face on television. He uses his fame to raise awareness of many important charities.

DAVID HAS A SELFIE TAKEN WITH ONE OF HIS FANS AT THE BRITAIN'S GOT TALENT AUDITIONS IN BIRMINGHAM IN 2015.

To raise money for the charity Comic Relief, in 2015 David wrote a book called The Queen's Orang-Utan. All the money from the sale of the book went to charity.

APPEARING ON BRITAIN'S GOT TALENT HAS MADE DAVID A HOUSEHOLD NAME.

DAVID ON FAME:

'WHEN YOU'RE WELL-KNOWN AND ON TELEVISION, IT'S PART OF YOUR LIFE THAT YOU'RE RECOGNISED. IT'S A VERY FORTUNATE POSITION YOU'RE IN.'

In 2011, David travelled to Kenya with Comic Relief. There, he met a young boy called Philip, who was living on the streets in dreadful conditions. David returned to Kenya in 2015 to see for himself how the charity's money was used. Philip was no longer living in the street. He was in school and studying.

DAVID ON MEETING PHILIP AGAIN:

'IT WAS INCREDIBLE TO SEE HOW HE'S CHANGED ... HE HAD SUCH A TOUGH LIFE BEFORE, UNIMAGINABLY HARD TO SOMEONE LIKE ME. AND NOW HE'S IN SUCH A BETTER PLACE AND I FEEL PROUD TO BE PART OF THAT.'

DAVID AND PROFESSOR STEPHEN HAWKING STARRED IN A SKETCH TOGETHER FOR COMIC RELIEF.

Although David and Matt decided not to make more episodes of *Little Britain*, in 2015, David played *Little Britain's* Lou for a charity special. Professor Stephen Hawking played the role of Andy, usually taken by Matt Lucas. What followed was a hilarious take on a comedy classic and helped Comic Relief to raise an eye-watering £78,000,000 that year.

Best seller

Always a keen and able writer, David has turned his hand to writing children's fiction. The comedian published his first book, *The Boy in the Dress*, in 2008. David's books have been translated into more than 40 languages, and have sold an amazing six million copies in the UK alone!

ASKED HOW HE COPES WITH WRITER'S BLOCK AND GETS INSPIRATION, DAVID SAYS:

'SOMETIMES JUST GETTING UP FROM THE DESK AND DOING SOMETHING DIFFERENT LIKE MAKING A CUP OF TEA HELPS YOUR BRAIN START WORKING AGAIN.'

Quentin Blake, who also illustrated many of Roald Dahl's books, illustrated both *The Boy in the Dress* and David's second book, *Mr Stink*.

DAVID ON ROALD DAHL:

'ROALD DAHL GOT ME HOOKED ON READING.'

Walliams' World

David is one of the most-read authors in UK schools. According to a survey of books that British children were reading in 2014, David was the fifth most-read author. David received the Children's Award in the People's Book Prize in 2010 for *Mr Stink*.

Since *Mr Stink*, David has written eight other novels for children, this time illustrated by Tony Ross. Both *Mr Stink* and *Gangsta Granny*, another of David's books, have also been made into television dramas. David is often compared to his literary hero, Roald Dahl, whose books he devoured when young.

ON *THE BOY IN THE DRESS*, DAVID SAYS:

'IT IS A FUNNY AND POIGNANT STORY ABOUT WHAT IT IS TO BE DIFFERENT. I HOPE IT WILL MAKE EVERYONE WHO SEES IT, YOUNG AND OLD, STOP AND THINK.'

Swimming for Success

David was honoured for his sporting endeavours when he received the BBC Sports Personality of the Year Special Award in 2006. This was in recognition of his Sport Relief swim across the English Channel. David's sporting undertakings for charity proved both his determination to help others and his fitness as a sportsman.

Training for months to prepare for his Channel swim, David sometimes endured eight-hour sessions in the chilly sea. On 4 July 2006, starting from a beach near Dover, David successfully swam the 35 kilometres across the English Channel in 10 hours 34 minutes. He covered himself in grease to keep warm and was given food from a pole on his support boat during the swim. David raised more than £1 million for the charity Sport Relief.

AN EXHAUSTED DAVID COMPLETES HIS RIVER THAMES SWIM AND IS HELPED FROM THE WATER.

In 2011, David swam 225 kilometres along the River Thames in an epic eight-day swim. His efforts raised more than £2 million for charity. During the swim, David rescued a drowning dog and suffered a serious tummy bug.

AFTER HIS RIVER THAMES SWIM, DAVID SAID:

'A BATH IS THE ONLY WATER I WANT TO SEE FOR QUITE A WHILE!'

ON THE JOHN O'GROATS BIKE CHALLENGE, DAVID REFLECTED:

'IT'S GOOD TO KEEP IN MIND WHO WE'RE HELPING. HOWEVER MUCH WE'RE MOANING, WE HAVE TO REMEMBER THAT'S THE REALITY OF PEOPLE'S LIVES ALL THE TIME ... OUR GROUP SUFFERING A TINY BIT PUTS THINGS INTO CONTEXT.'

In 2010, David and six other celebrities battled blizzards and freezing conditions as they took part in a non-stop relay cycle ride from John O'Groats to Land's End to raise money for charity. David fell as he struggled to gain speed to cycle up Kirkstone Pass – a 304-metre climb in the heart of the Lake District. Despite this accident, he and his fellow celebrities completed the gruelling charity ride.

Top Moments

Here is an overview of David's extraordinary life so far, including his numerous television shows and award-winning productions and publications:

1971: Born in Merton, London

1989: Starts National Youth Theatre

1989: Goes to Bristol University

1990: Meets Matt Lucas

1995: Performs at the Edinburgh Festival with Matt Lucas

1999: Stars with Matt Lucas in *Rock Profile*

2001: Records the first series of *Little Britain* for BBC's Radio 4

2003: Co-writes and stars in *Little Britain* for television

2006: Tours *Little Britain Live* with Matt Lucas

2006: Swims the English Channel for charity

2008: Publishes first children's book *The Boy in the Dress*

2010: Completes charity bike challenge

2010: Stars in *Come Fly With Me*

2011: Swims part of the River Thames for charity

2012: Becomes a presenter on *Britain's Got Talent*

2014: Co-hosts BBC *Sport Relief* for charity

Walliams' World

As an adult, David returned to Reigate Grammar School to make a television programme. The programme explored what had happened to the classmates who had been his ladies-in-waiting in the school play that inspired David's love of performance. The boys, now men, many of them living abroad, came together for a reunion.

Awards include:

2003: British Comedy Awards, Best TV Comedy Newcomer

2004: BAFTA TV Award for Best Comedy Programme, *Little Britain*

2005: BAFTA TV Award for Best Comedy Performance with Matt Lucas

Best Comedy Programme, *Little Britain*

2012: Landmark TV Award in recognition of swimming challenges for charity

2015: *Demon Dentist* wins Younger Reader's Award, The Red House Children's Book Award

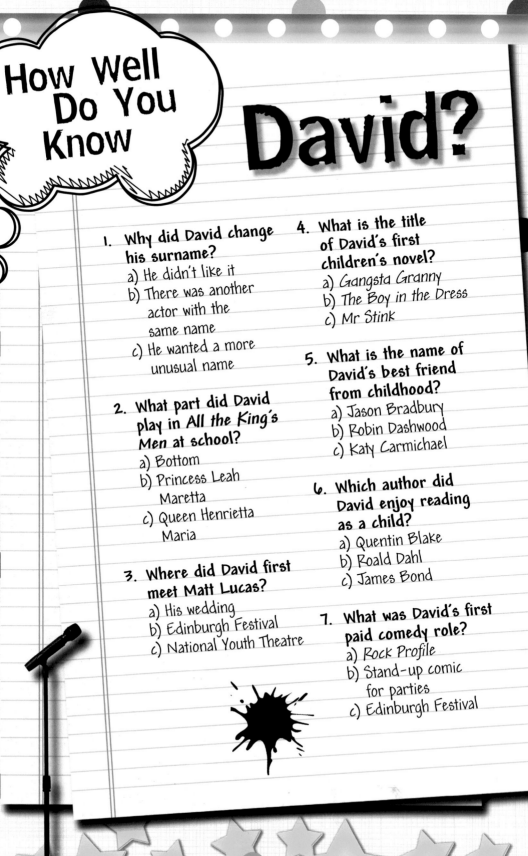

How Well Do You Know David?

1. **Why did David change his surname?**
   a) He didn't like it
   b) There was another actor with the same name
   c) He wanted a more unusual name

2. **What part did David play in All the King's Men at school?**
   a) Bottom
   b) Princess Leah Maretta
   c) Queen Henrietta Maria

3. **Where did David first meet Matt Lucas?**
   a) His wedding
   b) Edinburgh Festival
   c) National Youth Theatre

4. **What is the title of David's first children's novel?**
   a) Gangsta Granny
   b) The Boy in the Dress
   c) Mr Stink

5. **What is the name of David's best friend from childhood?**
   a) Jason Bradbury
   b) Robin Dashwood
   c) Katy Carmichael

6. **Which author did David enjoy reading as a child?**
   a) Quentin Blake
   b) Roald Dahl
   c) James Bond

7. **What was David's first paid comedy role?**
   a) Rock Profile
   b) Stand-up comic for parties
   c) Edinburgh Festival

8. How long did it take David to swim the English Channel?
   a) Eight days
   b) Eight hours 30 minutes
   c) 10 hours 34 minutes

9. Where did David cycle for Sport Relief in 2010?
   a) From London to Liverpool
   b) From Reigate to Bristol
   c) From John O'Groats to Land's End

10. When was David born?
   a) 1973
   b) 1961
   c) 1971

Answers

1. b) There was another actor with the same name
2. c) Queen Henrietta Maria
3. c) National Youth Theatre
4. b) *The Boy in the Dress*
5. b) Robin Dashwood
6. b) Roald Dahl
7. b) Stand-up comic for parties
8. c) 10 hours 34 minutes
9. c) From John O'Groats to Land's End
10. c) 1971

Find out more about David Walliams and his books at:
www.harpercollins.co.uk/cr-101054/david-walliams

Gain an insight into David's imagination by reading some of his books:
The Boy in the Dress
Mr Stink
Billionaire Boy
Gangsta Granny
Ratburger
Demon Dentist
Awful Auntie

Quote sources

Page 4 Camp David, 2012; **Page 7** www.whatsontv.co.uk; **Page 9** (top) Camp David, 2012, (bottom) Camp David, 2012; **Page 10** Radio Times, 2013; **Page 11** www.aworldatschool.org, 2014; **Page 12** Camp David, 2012; **Page 13** Camp David, 2012; **Page 15** Radio Times, 2013; **Page 17** http://news.bbc.co.uk; **Page 19** www.mirror.co.uk, 2013; **Page 20** Radio Times, 2013; **Page 21** www.rednoseday.com, 2015; **Page 22** worldofdavidwalliams.com; **Page 23** (top) www.radiotimes.com, 2014 (bottom) www.radiotimes.com, 2014; **Page 25** (top) www.bbc.co.uk, 2011, (bottom) www.bbc.co.uk, 2012

Glossary

alternative Different from a traditional version of something

civil engineer Someone who designs and checks structures such as bridges

collaboration Working together

comedy circuit Touring venues to perform comedy

devise To make up

Equity card Having an Equity card means a person is a member of the actors' union, Equity, and can then be employed as an actor

feats Achievements

inspiration Ideas that make someone want to do something

literary To do with books

personality The characteristics of a person, which determine how they are perceived by others

prestigious Well-respected

production company An organisation that makes films and television programmes

regally Royally

runner A helper during the making of a film or television programme

sketches Short performances

spoof Imitating something in a way that makes it funny

stand-up comedy When a comedian performs in front of an audience, and directly addresses them

toured Performed

venues Places for performance

voice-over A speaking part during a television show or advertisement, often providing a commentary about what is being seen by the viewer

Index